# PASSOVER

BY
HOWARD GREENFELD

ILLUSTRATED BY
ELAINE GROVE

DESIGNED
BY
BEA FEITLER

Holt, Rinehart and Winston
New York

Text Copyright © 1978 by Howard Greenfeld
Illustrations copyright © 1978 by Elaine Grove
Published simultaneously in Canada by Holt, Rinehart
and Winston of Canada, Limited.
Printed in the United States of America
10 9 8 7 6 5 4 3 2 1
Library of Congress Cataloging in Publication Data
Greenfeld, Howard.
    Passover.
    SUMMARY: A history of this 3000-year-old Jewish
holiday and an explanation of the Seder which commemorates
it.
    1. Passover — Juvenile literature. (1. Passover)
I. Grove, Elaine. II. Title.
BM695.P3G68      296.4'37      77-13910
ISBN 0-03-039921-1

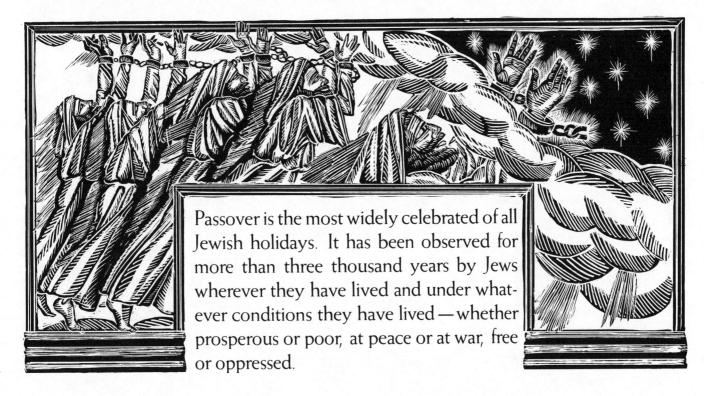

Passover is the most widely celebrated of all Jewish holidays. It has been observed for more than three thousand years by Jews wherever they have lived and under whatever conditions they have lived — whether prosperous or poor, at peace or at war, free or oppressed.

The reason this holiday has endured for so many centuries, without interruption, is that it celebrates a turning point in the history of the Jews, the time when they emerged as a free people after years of slavery in Egypt. It is a stirring festival of freedom, commemorating the birth of a community.

Jews, however, are not the only people who have been or still are oppressed, and for that reason this Jewish holiday has profound meaning for all. The story of Passover has universal significance. It is a dramatic reminder of the tragedy of slavery and the glory of freedom.

Toward the end of the *Seder* — the celebration which marks this holiday — the entrance door of each Jewish home is opened so that the prophet Elijah might enter. But another interpretation for this symbolic act, one which dates from the Middle Ages, is that the door is opened to allow outsiders — suspicious of all kinds of mysterious evildoings at a Seder — to enter and to learn the truth of what happens during this ceremonial meal.

This book is meant to be an opening of the door, so that all might learn the reasons for this holiday and the way in which it is celebrated.

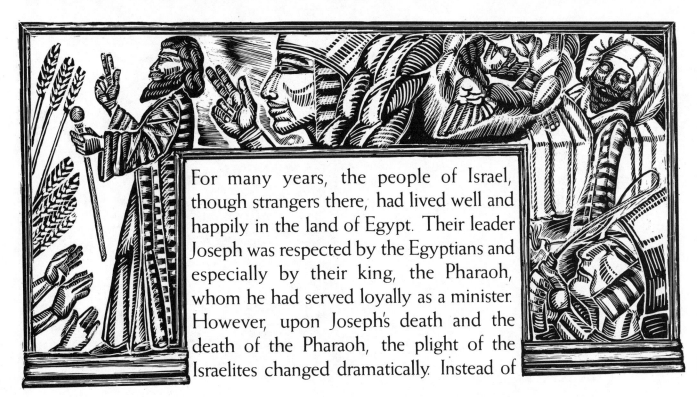

For many years, the people of Israel, though strangers there, had lived well and happily in the land of Egypt. Their leader Joseph was respected by the Egyptians and especially by their king, the Pharaoh, whom he had served loyally as a minister. However, upon Joseph's death and the death of the Pharaoh, the plight of the Israelites changed dramatically. Instead of

[7]

respecting these hard-working people who prospered and increased in his land, the new Pharaoh feared them. He was afraid that they might become too numerous and too powerful and that they were potentially strong enemies.

In order to weaken them, he first took measures to reduce their wealth. He taxed them heavily to make it impossible for them to grow rich and accumulate material goods. But this did not seem to go quite far enough. He took a more drastic step: he made them slaves. They were no longer free to live as they wanted or to work as [8] they wanted; instead, they were forced to

labor with mortar and bricks to build the treasure-filled cities of Pithom and Raamses for the Pharaoh. Life under this cruel, shrewd ruler was bitter for the Israelites. Nonetheless, the Israelite population continued to grow. To decrease the population, the Pharaoh decreed the harshest measure of all. Every male infant born to an Israelite was to be thrown into the Nile River and drowned. That would not only reduce the numbers of these people; it would also eliminate the danger predicted by Pharaoh's astrologers that one day an Israelite would be born who would free his people from their slavery in Egypt.

In time, however, such a leader was born. Defying the Pharaoh's decree, one Israelite mother refused to cast her infant son into the river. She hid him for three months, and when that was no longer safe she put him in a basket which she placed among the reeds along the bank of the Nile. The child's older sister kept watch from a distance to see what would happen.

Before long, the Pharaoh's daughter came down to bathe in the river and noticed the abandoned infant. Realizing that it must be an Israelite, she felt pity for the infant and decided to raise him as her own son. Before her servants carried the child away, the infant's sister approached her and volunteered to find an Israelite woman to act as the child's nurse. The Pharaoh's daughter accepted this offer, and in this way the infant's own mother was able to raise her own child. When he was older and brought to Pharaoh's daughter, she named him Moses.

Though he was raised in the palace of the Pharaoh, Moses knew that he was an Israelite and felt a bond with his own people as well as a profound anger for the injustices they suffered as slaves. It is not surprising then that one day, when grown, he became so enraged at the sight of an Egyptian

[11]

master brutally beating an Israelite that he killed the Egyptian. Fearing the punishment that would follow, he fled to the distant desert land of Midian.

Moses remained there for many years, until one day he came to the mountain of Horeb where he witnessed an astonishing sight. There was a bush completely surrounded by fire, but not burned by that fire. He approached it cautiously, and from the bush he heard the voice of God, saying that He had heard the plea for freedom uttered by the Israelites in Egypt, and that He would rescue them and see that they [12] were brought out of slavery —with Moses

as their leader. God then commanded Moses to return to Egypt and persuade Pharaoh to liberate the Israelites and allow them to leave the country.

Moses did as he was told and departed for Egypt. Time and again he went to the Pharaoh, pleading with him to free the Israelites. The Pharaoh not only refused, but made the life of the Israelites so much more difficult than ever, that Moses's own people begged him to stop trying to set them free.

Moses, however, persisted. He was determined to carry out the will of God and set his people free. When the Pharaoh, ignor-

[13]

ing Moses's warnings of the consequences, continued to deny freedom to the Israelites, God inflicted ten plagues upon the Egyptians and their country — plagues of *blood, frogs, lice, swarms of insects, pestilence, boils, hail and fire, locusts, darkness,* and *death to each firstborn child.* The first nine of these plagues caused great damage to the Egyptians, polluting their waters, destroying their lands and crops, killing their livestock, and causing physical pain to the people themselves. In spite of all this, the Pharaoh remained stubborn.

It was the tenth plague that broke his will.

The Lord was to visit the home of each Egyptian family and kill the firstborn child of that family. Only the Israelites would be spared. They had been told to sprinkle the blood of a lamb on the doorposts of their houses so that they would be recognized and passed over.

This plague would affect all the people of Egypt, including the Pharaoh's own family. Horrified at this prospect, he awoke one night and yielded to the will of God. He not only set the Israelites free, he ordered them out of Egypt at once. Word of Pharaoh's capitulation spread quickly, and the people of Israel hurriedly prepared their departure. Their haste was so great that there was not even time enough for the dough of the bread they were preparing to rise.

By morning, however, the Pharaoh had changed his mind. He realized that the loss of the slaves would severely weaken his country. . . and he sent soldiers and chariots after the Israelites to bring them back.

By the time the Egyptians came within reach of them, the Israelites were at the Red Sea. When they saw the troops approaching, they lost all hope. If they turned back, they would be captured by

the enemy and returned to slavery; if they went forward, they would be drowned in the sea.

Then what seemed a miracle occurred: as Moses raised his hands above the sea, a strong wind blew, parting the waters and allowing the Israelites to cross the sea by foot. The Egyptians and their chariots followed close behind, but as they crossed the sea, the wind changed. The waters were no longer divided. The pursuing Egyptians were drowned, and the people of Israel, led by Moses, at last were free. They had been redeemed by God, and for this they would be forever grateful.

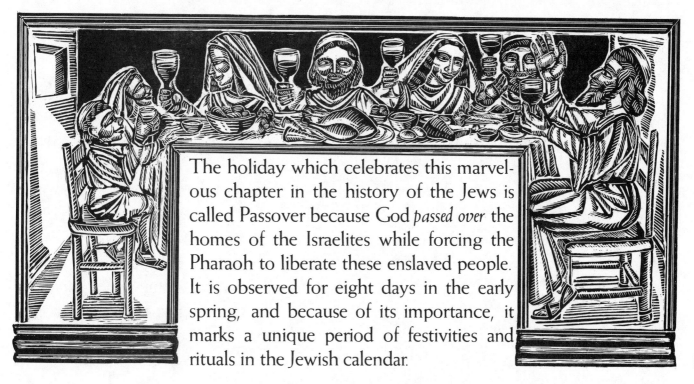

The holiday which celebrates this marvelous chapter in the history of the Jews is
called Passover because God *passed over* the
homes of the Israelites while forcing the
Pharaoh to liberate these enslaved people.
It is observed for eight days in the early
spring, and because of its importance, it
marks a unique period of festivities and
rituals in the Jewish calendar.

[17]

Before the holiday actually begins, careful preparations are made in the home. There is a thorough spring-cleaning — everything must shine and look new for the holiday season. Dishes and silverware and cooking utensils used the rest of the year are put aside and replaced by others which are used only during the eight days of Passover. Often, members of the family buy new clothing to wear during the festivities. Indeed, everything possible is done to show that this is a special time for every Jewish family.

Most important of all, every trace of [18] leavened food is removed from the home.

Leavened foods are the fermented products of grain (the list includes beer, most cakes, crackers, and bread).

During this season, bread is replaced by *matzah*, a crackerlike wafer made from dough which has not fermented and risen. This is a reminder to the Jewish people that their ancestors had to flee from Egypt in such a hurry that there was no time to bake their bread in the usual fashion.

Once the home has been prepared for the holiday, it is time for the Seder, the most beautiful and moving part of Passover. The word "Seder" means "order of service" in Hebrew, and this service is held in the

[19]

home, usually on the first two nights of the holiday.

The Seder is an occasion for prayer, for readings from the Bible, for reminding all those present of the meaning of this holiday, and for discussion and interpretation of that meaning. It is also a time for a festive meal, for company and high spirits. It is a time for rejoicing and pleasure, but, above all, it is a time for serious reflection on what happened when the Israelites were slaves and therefore a warning that this must never be permitted to happen again.

The table is lavishly set, as for a banquet, with the finest tablecloth and napkins, with candles, and with goblets for Passover wine. Prominently displayed on a richly decorated plate are those foods that symbolize the hardships of the Israelites during their slavery in Egypt. In the center of this plate are three pieces of matzah, wrapped in a special cloth or napkin; the middle piece will have a special meaning during the service. Around the matzah on the Seder plate are other reminders of the bondage and liberation of the Israelites. One of these, called *maror*, is a bitter herb, usually horseradish, to recall the bitter lives led under Egyptian domination. There is *haroset*, a mixture of crushed nuts and apples

[21]

and sweet spices combined with wine to make a kind of paste, which resembles in texture the mortar used to build the Pharaoh's cities. Also on the plate is a roasted shankbone of a lamb, the animal traditionally sacrificed at Passover in the days when the Israelites had their own temple. It is a reminder, too, of the blood of the lamb which marked the doorposts of the Israelites on the night the Pharaoh was forced to give them their freedom. Finally, there is a roasted egg, a symbol of life and growth and rebirth.

Also on the Seder plate—and on the table—are symbols of the springtime: sprigs of parsley, lettuce, or celery. These will be dipped in small bowls of salt water, which represents the tears shed in Egypt. There are also decanters filled with enough sweet red wine to allow each guest to drink four toasts to the ways in which the Israelites were liberated and redeemed by God. Finally, there is an extra wine glass for the prophet Elijah, who is expected to come after the meal to prepare the way for the Messiah, the deliverer.

On Seder night, the family gathers together. Relatives who might not have seen each other all year are united for this joyous occasion. They are often joined by friends

who do not have families of their own, for no one should be alone on Passover. With the leader, often seated on a cushion, at the head of the table, they take their places to begin this service and this meal that differs from all others throughout the year. Even their way of sitting is different, for instead of sitting erect in their chairs, they recline or lean as free men, at ease, did in ancient times.

The major purpose of the Seder is to recount the story of the liberation of the Israelites, their exodus from Egypt, and their redemption as a people by God, so that no Jew should ever forget the impor-

[23]

tance of these events and of freedom itself. The story is of particular importance to the young and must be passed on from generation to generation.

The story is found in the *Haggadah*, a book which is read aloud throughout the meal. "Haggadah" is a Hebrew word meaning "narration" and the book contains not only the story of the Israelites, but also the readings and rituals to be followed during the Seder. Each member of the family and each guest is given a Haggadah.

Different kinds of Haggadot are used in different homes, for there is no fixed or

official version. The texts, the biblical cita-

tions, the songs, the language used, and even the order of service vary from place to place, from generation to generation. Though the basic story of Passover remains the same, it is subject to an infinite number of interpretations. This very flexibility makes Passover a steadily interesting holiday, one which is forever alive and relevant, fresh and contemporary.

The full program for the Seder can be found in the Haggadah, but this summary of the high points of a typical Seder will give an idea of the memorable joys of these magical occasions.

Before the meal, there is a service which begins with the *Kiddush*, a prayer praising God for granting this festival of freedom. Then the leader dips the greens in the salt water and passes them around to be tasted by each participant. Next, he breaks the middle piece of matzah in half. One half, called the *Afikoman*, is hidden; toward the end of the evening the children will search for it. The other half of the matzah is held up for all to see, and the leader explains that it represents the bread of affliction and poverty. He then extends an invitation to all who are hungry to come and eat, setting the mood of warm hospitality that prevails throughout the holiday.

At this point, the youngest child at the Seder asks four questions: *Why is matzah eaten rather than bread? Why the bitter herbs? Why the dipping in salt water? Why are the guests reclining instead of sitting straight in their chairs?* In other words, the child wants to know why this night differs so from all other nights.

The answer for all to hear is, at first, a straightforward and simple one. "Our ancestors were slaves to the Pharaoh in Egypt but God brought us out from there. If it hadn't been for God, we would still be slaves."

The celebration of that extraordinary event is what makes the night of the Seder different from all others. And the story of that exodus from Egypt is told often so that it will never be forgotten. There are different ways of telling it and different levels on which it can be understood, and the Seder continues with brief comments about the different approaches which might be taken when telling the story to four sons — a wise son, a wicked son, a simple son, and a son who is too young even to ask about the story.

The story itself, based on biblical readings, follows. This is the main part of the service, and it is concerned with the transition of the Israelites from slavery to freedom, from

[27]

degradation to dignity, from the rule of evil to the Kingdom of God. This narration might be interrupted with discussions and digressions, and for contemporary interpretations. Anything of this nature has its place in a Seder. However, the celebrants are always reminded that in every generation an enemy has arisen to try to destroy the people of Israel, and that each time a divine power has sustained and saved them. At one point in the narration, each guest dips a finger into the wine glass and removes one drop of wine when each plague is mentioned, an act which symbolizes the lessening of joy when it is at-

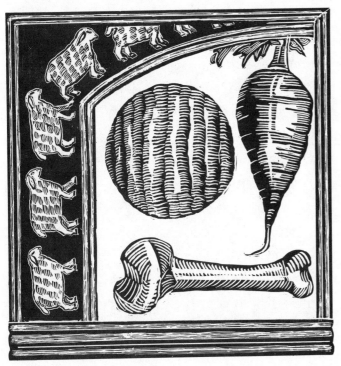

tained through the suffering of others — no matter who they are.

There follows a marvelous chant, a recital of the wondrous things God did for the Israelites. After each of these wonders is mentioned, the company says in unison: *Dayenu* — it would have been enough — the implication being that even only one of the miracles would have been sufficient reason to rejoice.

Once the story has been told and discussed, the three basic symbols — the matzah, the shankbone, and the bitter herbs — are explained. The bitter herbs are eaten with a little haroset (to sweeten them) on a piece [29]

of matzah, and it is time to begin the meal. Though it has been customary since Roman times to begin the Passover meal with a hard-boiled egg dipped in salt water, there is no traditional meal served at the Seder. The important thing is that it be an abundant dinner, worthy of a very special occasion.

Toward the end of the meal, the children begin to search for the Afikoman. Generally all those who have taken part in the search are rewarded when it is found, and a special prize is given to the finder. This piece of matzah is then divided among the guests and eaten. No food should be eaten after it, so that the taste of matzah remains in the mouth.

The meal ended, the door is opened to allow Elijah to enter and drink from his goblet. It is said that Elijah enters each Jewish home during the Seder, and the moment of the opening of the door should be a moment of suspense. Indeed, with the help of someone at the table, the wine that has been placed in his goblet sometimes "mysteriously" disappears.

There is more to come: psalms — hymns of praise to be recited, prayers to be chanted, and songs to be sung. The last part of the Seder is filled with gaiety, with jokes and

games and riddles. Then, at the conclusion of this memorable evening, the participants call out the traditional words of hope: "Next year in Jerusalem, next year may all men be free."

[31]

April 21 1978    Passover    14 Nisan 5738

    The typeface used in this book is Weiss Roman. The art was prepared in the scratchboard technique.